ENERGY BITES
FOR EVERYONE

Energy Bites for Everyone
English translation copyright © 2024 Robert Rose Inc.
Published originally in French (Canada) under the title *Le bonheur est dans les boules* © 2023 Guy Saint-Jean Éditeur inc.
Photographs copyright © Natercia Cabeceiras, except the photo on page 7 © 2020 AtlasStudio/Shutterstock
Cover and text design copyright © 2023 Guy Saint-Jean Éditeur inc.

No part of this publication may be reproduced, stored in a retrieval system or transmitted, in any form or by any means, without the prior written consent of the publisher or a licence from the Canadian Copyright Licensing Agency (Access Copyright). For an Access Copyright licence, visit www.accesscopyright.ca or call toll-free: 1-800-893-5777.

Library and Archives Canada Cataloguing in Publication
Title: Energy bites for everyone : 80 flavor bombs for the whole family / Sonia Lizotte.
Other titles: Bonheur est dans les boules. English
Names: Lizotte, Sonia, 1971- author.
Description: Translation of: Le bonheur est dans les boules. | Includes index.
Identifiers: Canadiana 20240338693 | ISBN 9780778807216 (softcover)
Subjects: LCSH: Snack foods. | LCSH: Desserts. | LCGFT: Cookbooks.
Classification: LCC TX740 .B6613 2024 | DDC 641.5/3—dc23

Design: Dorian Danielsen
Layout and Production: PageWave Graphics Inc.
Editor: Jennifer MacKenzie/Meredith Dees
Proofreader: Kelly Jones
Translator: Anne Louise Mahoney
Photography: Natercia Cabeceiras, except cookie scoop (page 7) © 2020 AtlasStudio/Shutterstock
Prop stylist: Sonia Lizotte

We acknowledge the support of the Government of Canada.

Canadä

Published by Robert Rose Inc.
120 Eglinton Avenue East, Suite 800, Toronto, Ontario, Canada M4P 1E2
Tel: (416) 322-6552 Fax: (416) 322-6936
www.robertrose.ca

Printed and bound in China

1 2 3 4 5 6 7 8 9 ESP 32 31 30 29 28 27 26 25 24

ENERGY BITES
FOR EVERYONE

80 Flavor Bombs for the Whole Family

Sonia Lizotte

Table of contents

Bites for All Appetites! — 6

Motivating Bites — 12

Delectable Bites — 54

Decadent Bites — 96

Surprising Bites — 140

Index — 184

Bites for ALL appetites!

Energy bites are nutritious and fortifying, rich in protein, fiber and carbohydrates. They require little effort in the kitchen even though they are super energizing. Plus, you can easily carry them in your purse, sports bag or backpack, so you can eat them anytime, anywhere!

These perfect snacks help overcome midafternoon slumps, allow active people to recharge their batteries before or after exercising and satisfy the cravings of kids and adults alike. They can even stand in for a quick breakfast when you're in a hurry. Say goodbye to often pricey store-bought bars that contain ingredients with questionable nutritional value!

Motivating bites PROVIDE ENERGY AND VITALITY AND ARE PARTNERS IN PHYSICAL ACTIVITY

Decadent bites MOVE YOU TO GIVE IN TO TEMPTATION WITH ZERO GUILT

Delectable bites OFFER PLENTY OF TASTE SENSATIONS AND EVOKE CHILDHOOD MEMORIES

Surprising bites INVITE YOU ON A JOURNEY WITH THEIR UNUSUAL AND UNIQUE FLAVORS

How to make the PERFECT BITES!

1 ADD **LIQUID** (WATER, MILK OR OTHER) IF THE MIXTURE IS TOO DRY OR ADD A **BINDER** (OATS, ALMOND FLOUR OR OTHER) IF IT IS TOO WET.

2 USE A **MEASURING SPOON** TO MAKE BALLS THAT ARE UNIFORM IN SIZE.

3 BEFORE SHAPING THE BALLS, **REFRIGERATE** THE MIXTURE IF THE CONSISTENCY IS TOO SOFT.

4 **WET** YOUR HANDS BEFORE SHAPING THE BALLS TO MAKE THE TASK EASIER.

Vanilla Cake

Makes around 8 cups (800 g) cake crumbs

🕐 15 minutes   📋 45 minutes   🗄 10 days   ❄ 3 months

Preparation

1. Preheat the oven to 350°F (180°C). Grease and flour a 13- by 9-inch (33 cm x 23 cm) baking pan.

2. In a bowl, mix the flour, baking powder and salt. Set aside.

3. In another bowl, using an electric mixer, beat the eggs and sugar for around 2 minutes, until the mixture lightens in color.

4. Add the oil and vanilla, mixing until combined.

5. Gradually add the dry ingredients, alternating with the milk. Pour batter into the prepared pan.

6. Bake for about 45 minutes, until a toothpick inserted in the center of the cake comes out clean.

7. Let the cake cool at room temperature for 1 hour. Using a fork, crumble the cake.

ONCE CRUMBLED, THIS VANILLA CAKE, AS WELL AS THE CHOCOLATE VERSION ON PAGE 11, FORM THE BASE FOR SEVERAL RECIPES IN THIS BOOK. IT IS ALSO DELICIOUS ICED WITH YOUR FAVORITE FROSTING!

Chocolate Cake

Makes around 8 cups (800 g) cake crumbs

🕐 15 minutes   📋 50 minutes   🗄 10 days   ❄ 3 months

Preparation

① Preheat the oven to 350° F (180° C). Grease and flour a 13- by 9-inch (33 cm x 23 cm) baking pan.

② In a bowl, mix the flour, cocoa powder, baking powder and salt. Set aside.

③ In another bowl, using an electric mixer, beat the butter, brown sugar and vanilla.

④ Add the eggs, one at a time, beating after each addition. Add the sour cream, mixing until combined.

⑤ Gradually add the dry ingredients, alternating with the milk. Pour batter into the prepared pan.

⑥ Bake for about 50 minutes, until a toothpick inserted in the center of the cake comes out clean.

⑦ Let the cake cool at room temperature for 1 hour. Using a fork, crumble the cake.

Motivating Bites

The bites in this section will give you some zip just when you need it, such as before a workout, while you do errands or during a hike, when fatigue creeps in. These blasts of energy will delight you from the very first bite.

Almond and Coconut • 15

Cereal and Dried Fruit • 17

Tahini, Date and Honey • 19

Multigrain • 21

Banana and Yogurt • 23

Sunflower Seed and Raisin • 25

Dried Apple and Cinnamon • 27

Granola and Cranberry • 29

Almond and Coconut

Makes around 24 bites

🕐 10 minutes   🗄 2 weeks   ❄ 3 months

Preparation

1. Place ½ cup (50 g) coconut in a shallow dish. Set aside.
2. In a food processor, process the almonds, 1 cup (100 g) coconut and the oats to a fine powder.
3. Add the honey and coconut oil and process until a ball forms.
4. Shape into balls, using about 1 tbsp of the mixture for each one. Coat evenly with the reserved coconut.

Cereal and Dried Fruit

Makes around 24 bites

🕐 15 minutes   🧊 2 weeks   ❄ 3 months

Preparation

1. In a bowl, coarsely crumble the corn flakes.
2. Add the remaining ingredients and mix well.
3. Shape into balls, using about 1 tbsp of the mixture for each one.

Tahini, Date and Honey

Makes around 30 bites

🕐 15 minutes   🗄 2 weeks   ❄ 3 months

Preparation

1. Using a knife, coarsely chop the dates and almonds.
2. In a large bowl, combine all the ingredients.
3. Shape into balls, using about 1 tbsp of the mixture for each one.

Multigrain

Makes around 24 bites

🕐 10 minutes   ▯ 2 weeks   ❄ 3 months

Preparation

① In a food processor, process all the ingredients until combined.

② Shape into balls, using about 1 tbsp of the mixture for each one.

Banana and Yogurt

Makes around 24 bites

🕐 10 minutes   🗄 2 weeks   ❄ 3 months

Preparation

1. In a bowl, combine all the ingredients.
2. Shape into balls, using about 1 tbsp of the mixture for each one.

Sunflower Seed and Raisin

Makes around 30 bites

🕐 10 minutes   📦 2 weeks   ❄ 3 months

Preparation

1. In a bowl, combine all the ingredients.
2. Shape into balls, using about 1 tbsp of the mixture for each one.

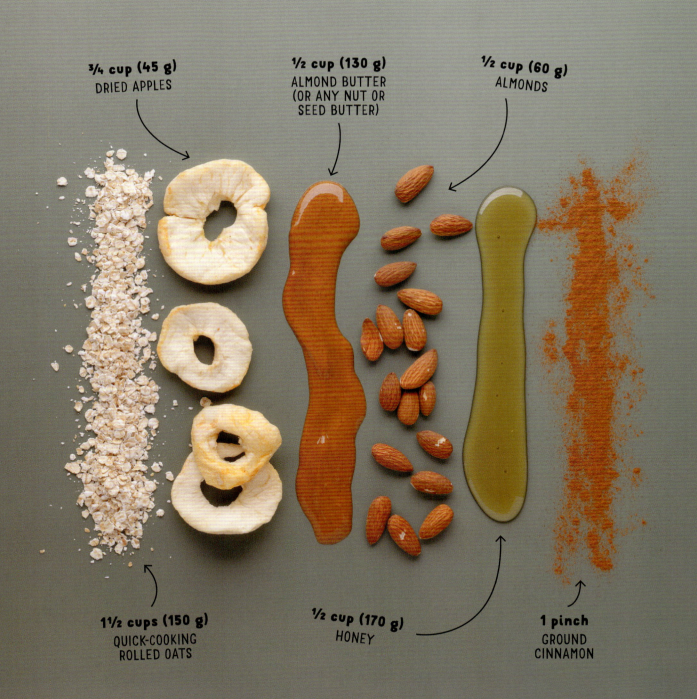

Dried Apple and Cinnamon

Makes around 24 bites

🕐 15 minutes   🗄 2 weeks   ❄ 3 months

Preparation

1. Using a knife, coarsely chop the almonds and dried apples.
2. In a bowl, combine all the ingredients.
3. Shape into balls, using about 1 tbsp of the mixture for each one.

Granola and Cranberry

Makes around 24 bites

⏰ 10 minutes   🗄 2 weeks   ❄ 3 months

Preparation

1. In a bowl, combine all the ingredients.
2. Shape into balls, using about 1 tbsp of the mixture for each one.

Oat and Apricot

Makes around 24 bites

🕐 15 minutes   🗄 2 weeks   ❄ 3 months

Preparation

1. Using a knife, coarsely chop the cashews and apricots.
2. In a bowl, combine all the ingredients.
3. Shape into balls, using about 1 tbsp of the mixture for each one.

Pecan and Coffee

Makes around 24 bites

🕐 10 minutes 🧊 2 weeks ❄ 3 months

Preparation

1. In a bowl, combine all the ingredients.
2. Shape into balls, using about 1 tbsp of the mixture for each one.

Toasted Sesame Seed and Dark Chocolate

Makes around 24 bites

🕐 15 minutes   🗄 2 weeks   ❄ 3 months

Preparation

1. Place the toasted sesame seeds in a shallow dish. Set aside.
2. In a bowl, combine the remaining ingredients.
3. Shape into balls, using about 1 tbsp of the mixture for each one. Coat evenly with the toasted sesame seeds.

To Toast Sesame Seeds

In a nonstick skillet, over medium-high heat, toast the sesame seeds, stirring constantly, for about 3 minutes, until golden brown.

Pistachio and Pumpkin Seed

Makes around 24 bites

🕐 10 minutes   🗄 2 weeks   ❄ 3 months

Preparation

1. In a food processor, process all the ingredients until combined.
2. Shape into balls, using about 1 tbsp of the mixture for each one.

¼ cup (65 g)
ALMOND BUTTER

2½ cups (250 g)
QUICK-COOKING
ROLLED OATS

½ cup (60 g)
ALMOND FLOUR

¼ cup (30 g)
GROUND FLAXSEED

¾ cup (110 g)
FRESH BLUEBERRIES

½ cup (170 g)
HONEY

Blueberry Flaxseed

Makes around 24 bites

🕐 10 minutes   🗄 2 weeks   ❄ 3 months

Preparation

1. In a food processor, process all the ingredients until combined.
2. Shape into balls, using about 1 tbsp of the mixture for each one.

Whole Grain and Dried Pineapple

Makes around 24 bites

🕐 10 minutes   📦 2 weeks   ❄ 3 months

Preparation

1. In a food processor, process all the ingredients until combined.
2. Shape into balls, using about 1 tbsp of the mixture for each one.

Date and Chia Seed

Makes around 30 bites

⏱ 10 minutes   🗄 2 weeks   ❄ 3 months

Preparation

1. In a food processor, process the peanut butter, chia seeds, oats and dates until combined.
2. Stir in the peanuts and chocolate chips by hand.
3. Shape into balls, using about 1 tbsp of the mixture for each one.

43

Pumpkin Seed and Dried Kiwi

Makes around 30 bites

⏲ 10 minutes   🗄 2 weeks   ❄ 3 months

Preparation

1. In a bowl, combine all the ingredients.
2. Shape into balls, using about 1 tbsp of the mixture for each one.

Trail Mix

Makes around 24 bites

⏱ 10 minutes   🧊 2 weeks   ❄ 3 months

Preparation

1. In a food processor, process all the ingredients until combined.
2. Shape into balls, using about 1 tbsp of the mixture for each one.

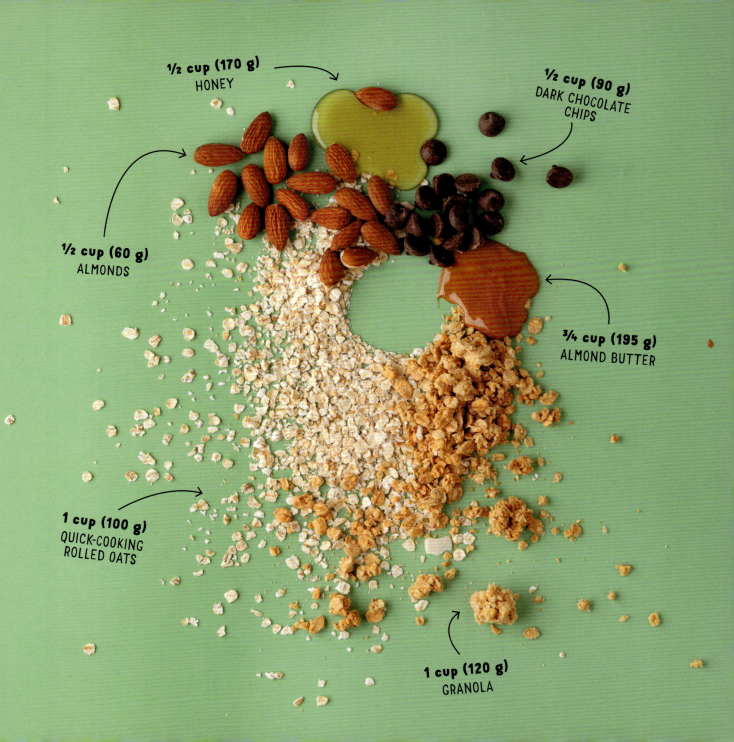

Dark Chocolate Almond

Makes around 32 bites

🕐 15 minutes   🗄 2 weeks   ❄ 3 months

Preparation

1. Using a knife, coarsely chop the almonds.
2. In a bowl, combine all the ingredients.
3. Shape into balls, using about 1 tbsp of the mixture for each one.

Raspberry Coconut

Makes around 24 bites

🕐 10 minutes   📦 2 weeks   ❄ 3 months

Preparation

① In a food processor, process all the ingredients until combined.

② Shape into balls, using about 1 tbsp of the mixture for each one.

Three Nut and Creamed Honey

Makes around 32 bites

- 10 minutes
- 2 weeks
- 3 months

Preparation

1. In a food processor, process all the ingredients until combined.
2. Shape into balls, using about 1 tbsp of the mixture for each one.

Delectable Bites

These bites will please your senses and delight your inner child.
Playful and comforting, they'll put a smile on your face.

Chocolate Chip • 57
Marble • 59
Banana Bread • 61
Choco-Peanut Butter • 63
Almost-a-Bear-Claw • 65
Vanilla Berry • 67
Pistachio Mint • 69
Lemon Poppy Seed • 71

Chocolate Chip

Makes around 24 bites

🕐 10 minutes   🗄 2 weeks   ❄ 3 months

Preparation

1. In a food processor, process the oats to a fine powder.
2. Add the remaining ingredients except the chocolate chips.
3. Add the water, 1 tbsp at a time, and process until the mixture forms a ball. It should resemble the consistency of cookie dough.
4. Place in a bowl and stir in the chocolate chips.
5. Shape into balls, using about 1 tbsp of the mixture for each one.

Marble

Makes around 24 bites

🕐 15 minutes   📦 2 weeks   ❄ 3 months

Preparation

1. In a food processor, process the oats to a fine powder.
2. Add the remaining ingredients except the cocoa powder and chocolate chips.
3. Add the water, 1 tbsp at a time, and process until the mixture forms a ball. It should resemble the consistency of cookie dough.
4. Place half the mixture in a bowl. Stir in the white chocolate chips.
5. Add the cocoa powder to the food processor and process until combined. Place mixture in another bowl and stir in the dark chocolate chips.
6. Gently combine the two mixtures, swirling with a knife, to create a marbled effect.
7. Shape into balls, using about 1 tbsp of the mixture for each one.

Cold water
TO MOISTEN THE MIXTURE

½ cup (125 g)
MASHED BANANA

2½ cups (250 g)
QUICK-COOKING
ROLLED OATS

½ cup (135 g)
CASHEW BUTTER

3 tbsp (57 g)
CARAMEL SAUCE

½ cup (60 g)
WALNUTS, COARSELY
CHOPPED

¼ cup (30 g)
GROUND FLAXSEED

Banana Bread

Makes around 24 bites

🕐 10 minutes 🧊 2 weeks ❄ 3 months

Preparation

1. In a food processor, process the oats to a fine powder.
2. Add the remaining ingredients except the walnuts.
3. Add the water, 1 tbsp at a time, and process until the mixture forms a ball. It should resemble the consistency of cookie dough.
4. Place in a bowl and stir in the walnuts.
5. Shape into balls, using about 1 tbsp of the mixture for each one.

Choco-Peanut Butter

Makes around 24 bites

🕐 15 minutes   🗄 2 weeks   ❄ 3 months

Preparation

1. Place the cocoa powder in a shallow dish. Set aside.
2. In a food processor, process the oats to a fine powder.
3. Add the remaining ingredients except the chocolate chips.
4. Add the water, 1 tbsp at a time, and process until the mixture forms a ball. It should resemble the consistency of cookie dough.
5. Place in a bowl and stir in the chocolate chips.
6. Shape into balls, using about 1 tbsp of the mixture for each one. Coat evenly with cocoa powder.

Almost-a-Bear-Claw

Makes around 24 bites

🕐 10 minutes   🗄 2 weeks   ❄ 3 months

Preparation

1. In a food processor, process the corn flakes to a fine powder.
2. Add the remaining ingredients.
3. Add the water, 1 tbsp at a time, and process until the mixture forms a ball. It should resemble the consistency of cookie dough.
4. Shape into balls, using about 1 tbsp of the mixture for each one.

Vanilla Berry

Makes around 24 bites

🕐 10 minutes   📦 2 weeks   ❄ 3 months

Preparation

1. In a food processor, process the oats to a fine powder.
2. Add the remaining ingredients.
3. Add the water, 1 tbsp at a time, and process until the mixture forms a ball. It should resemble the consistency of cookie dough.
4. Shape into balls, using about 1 tbsp of the mixture for each one.

Pistachio Mint

Makes around 20 bites

🕐 10 minutes   🗄 2 weeks   ❄ 3 months

Preparation

1. In a food processor, process the oats to a fine powder.
2. Add the remaining ingredients.
3. Add the water, 1 tbsp at a time, and process until the mixture forms a ball. It should resemble the consistency of cookie dough.
4. Shape into balls, using about 1 tbsp of the mixture for each one.

Lemon Poppy Seed

Makes around 24 bites

⏲ 10 minutes   🗄 2 weeks   ❄ 3 months

Preparation

1. In a food processor, process the oats to a fine powder.
2. Add the remaining ingredients.
3. Add the water, 1 tbsp at a time, and process until the mixture forms a ball. It should resemble the consistency of cookie dough.
4. Shape into balls, using about 1 tbsp of the mixture for each one.

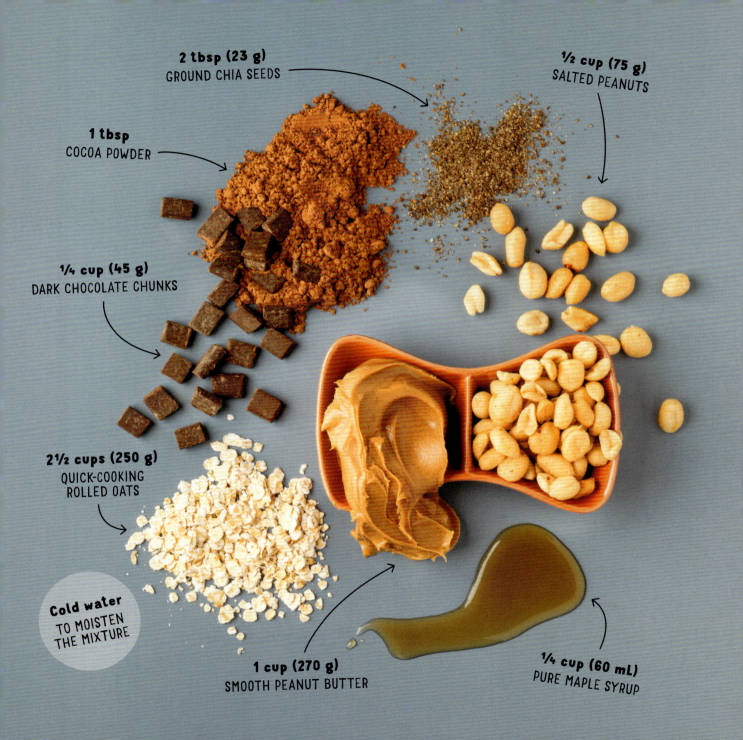

Crunchy Peanut

Makes around 24 bites

🕐 10 minutes   🗄 2 weeks   ❄ 3 months

Preparation

1. In a food processor, process the oats to a fine powder.
2. Add the remaining ingredients except the peanuts.
3. Add the water, 1 tbsp at a time, and process until the mixture forms a ball. It should resemble the consistency of cookie dough.
4. Place in a bowl and add the peanuts.
5. Shape into balls, using about 1 tbsp of the mixture for each one.

Graham Cracker

Makes around 24 bites

🕐 10 minutes   📦 2 weeks   ❄ 3 months

Preparation

1. Place all the ingredients in a food processor.
2. Add the water, 1 tbsp at a time, and process until the mixture forms a ball. It should resemble the consistency of cookie dough.
3. Shape into balls, using about 1 tbsp of the mixture for each one.

Toasted Coconut

Makes around 24 bites

🕐 15 minutes   📦 2 weeks   ❄ 3 months

Preparation

1. Place ½ cup (50 g) coconut in a shallow dish. Set aside.
2. Place all the remaining ingredients in a food processor.
3. Add the water, 1 tbsp at a time, and process until the mixture forms a ball. It should resemble the consistency of cookie dough.
4. Shape into balls, using about 1 tbsp of the mixture for each one. Coat evenly with coconut.

Crunchy Fudge

Makes around 36 bites

🕐 10 minutes   📦 2 weeks   ❄ 3 months

Preparation

1. In a food processor, process all the ingredients except the walnuts.
2. Add the water, 1 tbsp at a time, and process until the mixture forms a ball. It should resemble the consistency of cookie dough.
3. Place in a bowl and stir in the walnuts.
4. Shape into balls, using about 1 tbsp of the mixture for each one.

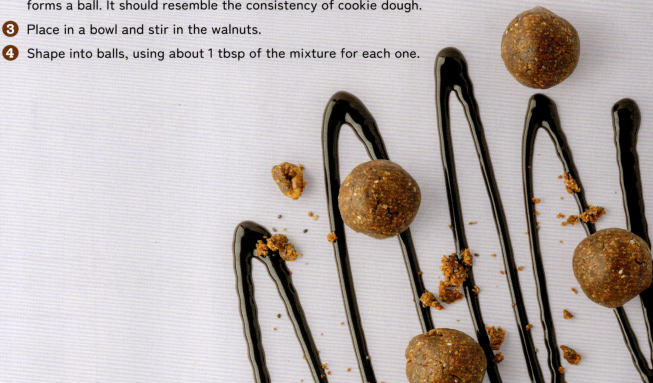

Cinnamon Bun

Makes around 24 bites

🕐 10 minutes   🧊 2 weeks   ❄ 3 months

Preparation

1. In a food processor, process all the ingredients.
2. Add the water, 1 tbsp at a time, and process until the mixture forms a ball. It should resemble the consistency of cookie dough.
3. Shape into balls, using about 1 tbsp of the mixture for each one.

Berry Center

Makes around 30 bites

🕐 15 minutes   📦 10 days   ❄ 3 months

Preparation

1. In a food processor, process all the ingredients except the Swedish Berries.
2. Add the water, 1 tbsp at a time, and process until the mixture forms a ball. It should resemble the consistency of cookie dough.
3. Shape into balls, using about 1 tbsp of the mixture for each. Position each ball in the palm of your hand and make a well in the center with your thumb. Place a Swedish Berry inside and close up the ball.

Old-Fashioned Donut

Makes around 24 bites

⏲ 10 minutes   📦 2 weeks   ❄ 3 months

Preparation

1. In a food processor, process all the ingredients.
2. Add the water, 1 tbsp at a time, and process until the mixture forms a ball. It should resemble the consistency of cookie dough.
3. Shape into balls, using about 1 tbsp of the mixture for each one.

Strawberry Jam

Makes around 24 bites

🕐 10 minutes   📅 10 days   ❄ 3 months

Preparation

1. In a food processor, process all the ingredients.
2. Add the water, 1 tbsp at a time, and process until the mixture forms a ball. It should resemble the consistency of cookie dough.
3. Shape into balls, using about 1 tbsp of the mixture for each one.

Fluffy Blueberry

Makes around 24 bites

🕐 10 minutes   📦 2 weeks   ❄ 3 months

Preparation

1. Place all the ingredients in a food processor.
2. Add the water, 1 tbsp at a time, and process until the mixture forms a ball. It should resemble the consistency of cookie dough.
3. Shape into balls, using about 1 tbsp of the mixture for each one.

Cherry Yogurt

Makes around 24 bites

🕐 10 minutes   🗄 2 weeks   ❄ 3 months

Preparation

1. In a food processor, process the oats to a fine powder.
2. Add the remaining ingredients.
3. Add the water, 1 tbsp at a time, and process until the mixture forms a ball. It should resemble the consistency of cookie dough.
4. Shape into balls, using about 1 tbsp of the mixture for each one.

Hot Chocolate

Makes around 24 bites

⏱ 15 minutes   🗄 2 weeks   ❄ 3 months

Preparation

1. Place ¼ cup (50 g) hot chocolate powder in a shallow dish. Set aside.
2. In a food processor, process the corn flakes to a fine powder.
3. Add the remaining ingredients except the milk.
4. Add milk, 1 tbsp at a time, and process until the mixture forms a ball. It should resemble the consistency of cookie dough.
5. Shape into balls, using about 1 tbsp of the mixture for each one. Coat evenly with hot chocolate powder.

Puffed Rice and Marshmallow

Makes around 20 bites

🕐 10 minutes   📦 2 weeks   ❄ 3 months

Preparation

1. In a food processor, pulse the almonds until coarsely chopped.
2. Add the remaining ingredients.
3. Add the water, 1 tbsp at a time, and process until the mixture forms a ball. It should resemble the consistency of cookie dough.
4. Shape into balls, using about 1 tbsp of the mixture for each one.

Decadent Bites

These bites stand out thanks to their irresistible flavors. You can also enjoy them as little desserts after a meal to satisfy a sweet tooth.

Black Forest • 99
Dulce de Leche • 101
Cheesecake • 103
Chocolate Brownie • 105
Carrot Cake • 107
Pecan Pie • 109
Baileys Coffee • 111
Key Lime Pie • 113
Rum Baba • 115

Black Forest

Makes around 30 bites

🕐 15 minutes   📦 2 weeks   ❄ 3 months

Preparation

1. Place all the ingredients except the chocolate wafers in a food processor.
2. Add the water, 1 tbsp at a time, and process until the mixture forms a ball. It should resemble the consistency of cookie dough.
3. Shape into balls, using about 1 tbsp of the mixture for each one. Place in the freezer for 15 minutes.
4. Place the chocolate wafers in a bowl, then melt in the microwave on High, for 2 to 5 minutes, depending on the microwave.
5. Coat the balls evenly in melted chocolate, then refrigerate until the chocolate has completely hardened before serving, about 10 minutes.

Dulce de Leche

Makes around 30 bites

🕒 15 minutes 📦 2 weeks ❄ 3 months

Preparation

1. In a food processor, process the oats to a fine powder.
2. Add the cake crumbs, cashew butter and dulce de leche.
3. Add the water, 1 tbsp at a time, and process until the mixture forms a ball. It should resemble the consistency of cookie dough.
4. Place in a bowl and add the cashews.
5. Shape into balls, using about 1 tbsp of the mixture for each one.

Cheesecake

Makes around 30 bites

🕐 10 minutes   ▭ 2 weeks   ❄ 3 months

Preparation

1. In a food processor, process all the ingredients until combined.
2. Add the water, 1 tbsp at a time, and process until the mixture forms a ball. It should resemble the consistency of cookie dough.
3. Shape into balls, using about 1 tbsp of the mixture for each one.

Chocolate Brownie

Makes around 30 bites

⏲ 15 minutes   📦 2 weeks   ❄ 3 months

Preparation

1. Place all the ingredients except the walnuts and chocolate chips in a food processor.
2. Add the water, 1 tbsp at a time, and process until the mixture forms a ball. It should resemble the consistency of cookie dough.
3. Place in a bowl, then stir in the walnuts and chocolate chips.
4. Shape into balls, using about 1 tbsp of the mixture for each one.

Carrot Cake

Makes around 24 bites

🕐 15 minutes   📦 2 weeks   ❄ 3 months

Preparation

1. Place all the ingredients except the walnuts in a food processor.
2. Add the water, 1 tbsp at a time, and process until the mixture forms a ball. It should resemble the consistency of cookie dough.
3. Place in a bowl, then stir in the walnuts.
4. Shape into balls, using about 1 tbsp of the mixture for each one.

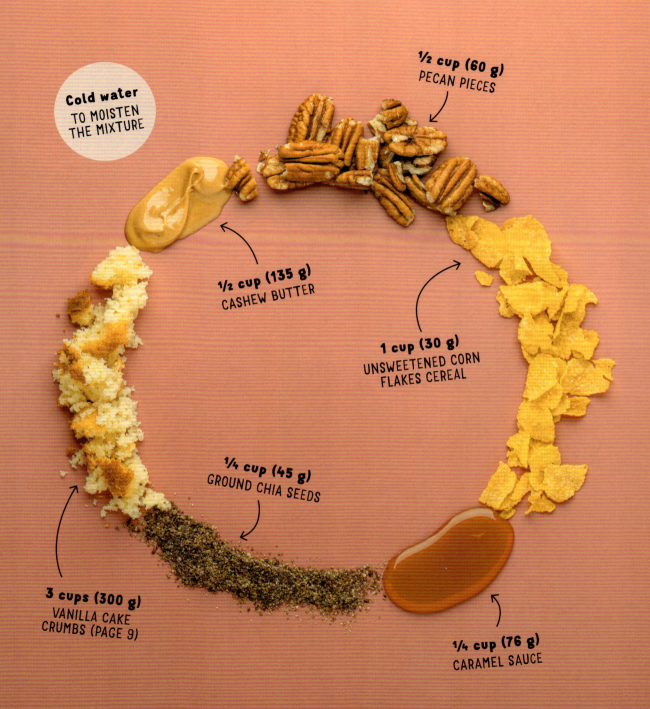

Pecan Pie

Makes around 24 bites

🕐 15 minutes   📦 2 weeks   ❄ 3 months

Preparation

1. In a food processor, process the corn flakes to a fine powder.
2. Add the remaining ingredients except the pecans.
3. Add the water, 1 tbsp at a time, and process until the mixture forms a ball. It should resemble the consistency of cookie dough.
4. Place in a bowl, then stir in the pecans.
5. Shape into balls, using about 1 tbsp of the mixture for each one.

Baileys Coffee

Makes around 24 bites

⏱ 10 minutes   🗄 2 weeks   ❄ 3 months

Preparation

1. In a food processor, process all the ingredients until combined.
2. Add the water or Baileys, 1 tbsp at a time, and process until the mixture forms a ball. It should resemble the consistency of cookie dough.
3. Shape into balls, using about 1 tbsp of the mixture for each one.

Key Lime Pie

Makes around 24 bites

🕐 10 minutes 🗄 2 weeks ❄ 3 months

Preparation

① In a food processor, process all the ingredients until combined.

② Add the water, 1 tbsp at a time, and process until the mixture forms a ball. It should resemble the consistency of cookie dough.

③ Shape into balls, using about 1 tbsp of the mixture for each one.

Rum Baba

Makes around 24 bites

⏲ 10 minutes   🗄 2 weeks   ❄ 3 months

Preparation

① In a food processor, process all the ingredients until combined.

② Add the water, 1 tbsp at a time, and process until the mixture forms a ball. It should resemble the consistency of cookie dough.

③ Shape into balls, using about 1 tbsp of the mixture for each one.

Choco-Sour Cream

Makes around 24 bites

⏱ 15 minutes 📦 2 weeks ❄ 3 months

Preparation

1. Place all the ingredients except the chocolate chips in a food processor.
2. Add the water, 1 tbsp at a time, and process until the mixture forms a ball. It should resemble the consistency of cookie dough.
3. Place in a bowl, then stir in the chocolate chips.
4. Shape into balls, using about 1 tbsp of the mixture for each one.

Piña Colada

Makes around 30 bites

⏱ 15 minutes   🗄 2 weeks   ❄ 3 months

Preparation

1. Place the coconut in a shallow dish. Set aside.
2. In a food processor, process the remaining ingredients until combined.
3. Add the water, 1 tbsp at a time, and process until the mixture forms a ball. It should resemble the consistency of cookie dough.
4. Shape into balls, using about 1 tbsp of the mixture for each one. Coat evenly with the coconut.

Cashew and Pretzel

Makes around 24 bites

🕐 15 minutes   📦 2 weeks   ❄ 3 months

Preparation

1. Place all the ingredients except the cashews and pretzels in a food processor.
2. Add the water, 1 tbsp at a time, and process until the mixture forms a ball. It should resemble the consistency of cookie dough.
3. Place in a bowl, then stir in the cashews and pretzels.
4. Shape into balls, using about 1 tbsp of the mixture for each one.

Oreo Swirl

Makes around 24 bites

🕐 15 minutes   📦 2 weeks   ❄ 3 months

Preparation

1. Place all the ingredients except the Oreo cookies in a food processor.
2. Add the water, 1 tbsp at a time, and process until the mixture forms a ball. It should resemble the consistency of cookie dough.
3. Place in a bowl, then stir in the chopped Oreos.
4. Shape into balls, using about 1 tbsp of the mixture for each one.

Double Chocolate

Makes around 30 bites

🕐 20 minutes   🗄 10 days   ❄ 3 months

Preparation

1. Place all the ingredients except the chocolate wafers in a food processor.
2. Add the water, 1 tbsp at a time, and process until the mixture forms a ball. It should resemble the consistency of cookie dough.
3. Put the chocolate wafers in a bowl, then melt in the microwave on High, for 2 to 5 minutes, depending on the microwave.
4. Shape into balls, using about 1 tbsp of the mixture for each one. Place in the freezer for 15 minutes.
5. Coat half of each ball in melted chocolate. Refrigerate until the chocolate has completely hardened before serving, about 10 minutes.

Red Velvet

Makes around 24 bites

🕐 10 minutes 🗄 2 weeks ❄ 3 months

Preparation

① In a food processor, process all the ingredients until combined.

② Add the water, 1 tbsp at a time, and process until the mixture forms a ball. It should resemble the consistency of cookie dough.

③ Shape into balls, using about 1 tbsp of the mixture for each one.

Strawberry Shortcake

Makes around 30 bites

🕐 15 minutes   📦 10 days   ❄ 3 months

Preparation

1. Place all the ingredients except the chocolate chips in a food processor.
2. Add the water, 1 tbsp at a time, and process until the mixture forms a ball. It should resemble the consistency of cookie dough.
3. Place in a bowl, then stir in the chocolate chips.
4. Shape into balls, using about 1 tbsp of the mixture for each one.

Cold water TO MOISTEN THE MIXTURE

20 SQUARES CARAMILK CHOCOLATE (FROM TWO 1.8 OZ/50 G BARS)

2 cups (200 g) CHOCOLATE CAKE CRUMBS (PAGE 11)

3 cups (90 g) UNSWEETENED CORN FLAKES CEREAL

½ cup (135 g) SMOOTH PEANUT BUTTER

¼ cup (30 g) GROUND FLAXSEED

Caramel Center

Makes around 20 bites

🕐 15 minutes   📦 2 weeks   ❄ 3 months

Preparation

① Place all the ingredients except the chocolate squares in a food processor.

② Add the water, 1 tbsp at a time, and process until the mixture forms a ball. It should resemble the consistency of cookie dough.

③ Shape into balls, using about 1 tbsp of the mixture for each one. Position each ball in the palm of your hand and make a well in the center with your thumb. Place a square of chocolate inside and close up the ball.

Ice Cream

Makes around 20 bites

⏱ 15 minutes   ▯ 2 weeks   ❄ 3 months

Preparation

1. Place all the ingredients except the chocolate chips in a food processor.
2. Add the water, 1 tbsp at a time, and process until the mixture forms a ball. It should resemble the consistency of cookie dough.
3. Place in a bowl, then stir in the chocolate chips.
4. Shape into balls, using about 1 tbsp of the mixture for each one.

Lemon Pie

Makes around 24 bites

🕐 10 minutes   📦 2 weeks   ❄ 3 months

Preparation

1. In a food processor, process all the ingredients until combined.
2. Add the water, 1 tbsp at a time, and process until the mixture forms a ball. It should resemble the consistency of cookie dough.
3. Shape into balls, using about 1 tbsp of the mixture for each one.

Cotton Candy

Makes around 30 bites

🕐 10 minutes   📦 2 weeks   ❄ 3 months

Preparation

1. In a food processor, process all the ingredients until combined.
2. Add the water, 1 tbsp at a time, and process until the mixture forms a ball. It should resemble the consistency of cookie dough.
3. Shape into balls, using about 1 tbsp of the mixture for each one.

Caramel and Fleur de Sel

Makes around 30 bites

⏲ 15 minutes   🧊 2 weeks   ❄ 3 months

Preparation

1. In a nonstick skillet, over medium-high heat, toast the almonds, stirring constantly, for 2 minutes, until browned.
2. Place the almonds in a food processor. Add the remaining ingredients except the fleur de sel.
3. Add the water, 1 tbsp at a time, and process until the mixture forms a ball. It should resemble the consistency of cookie dough.
4. Add the fleur de sel and stir to combine.
5. Shape into balls, using about 1 tbsp of the mixture for each one.

Surprising Bites

The bites in this section invite you on a stroll through your taste sensations.
You'll be surprised by the combination of unexpected ingredients.
Open yourself up to new horizons as you discover new textures and unfamiliar flavors.

Tofu and Toasted Sesame Seed • 143

Tempeh and Molasses • 147

Tofu Maple Walnut • 145

Lentil and Butterscotch Chip • 153

Tempeh and Maple Butter • 149

White Bean and Cocoa • 151

Zucchini and Dark Chocolate • 159

Honey Nut • 155

Quinoa and Crunchy Peanut Butter • 157

141

Tofu and Toasted Sesame Seed

Makes around 32 bites

⏱ 15 minutes   📦 1 week   ❄ 3 months

Preparation

1. Place the toasted sesame seeds in a shallow dish. Set aside.
2. In a food processor, process the remaining ingredients until combined.
3. Shape into balls, using about 1 tbsp of the mixture for each one. Coat evenly with toasted sesame seeds.

Tofu Maple Walnut

Makes around 24 bites

🕐 10 minutes   📦 1 week   ❄ 3 months

Preparation

1. In a bowl, combine all the ingredients.
2. Shape into balls, using about 1 tbsp of the mixture for each one.

Tempeh and Molasses

Makes around 30 bites

🕙 10 minutes   🗄 1 week   ❄ 3 months

Preparation

1. In a bowl, combine all the ingredients.
2. Shape into balls, using about 1 tbsp of the mixture for each one.

Tempeh and Maple Butter

Makes around 30 bites

🕐 10 minutes   📦 1 week   ❄ 3 months

Preparation

1. In a bowl, combine all the ingredients.
2. Shape into balls, using about 1 tbsp of the mixture for each one.

White Bean and Cocoa

Makes around 24 bites

🕐 15 minutes   📦 2 weeks   ❄ 3 months

Preparation

1. Place the cocoa powder in a shallow dish. Set aside.
2. In a food processor, process the remaining ingredients until combined.
3. Add the water, 1 tbsp at a time, and process until the mixture forms a ball. It should resemble the consistency of cookie dough.
4. Shape into balls, using about 1 tbsp of the mixture for each one. Coat evenly with cocoa powder.

Lentil and Butterscotch Chip

Makes around 30 bites

🕐 15 minutes   🗄 2 weeks   ❄ 3 months

Preparation

1. In a food processor, process all the ingredients except the butterscotch chips until combined.
2. Pour into a bowl, then stir in the butterscotch chips.
3. Shape into balls, using about 1 tbsp of the mixture for each one.

Honey Nut

Makes around 20 bites

🕐 10 minutes   📦 2 weeks   ❄ 3 months

Preparation

1. In a food processor, process all the ingredients until combined.
2. Shape into balls, using about 1 tbsp of the mixture for each one.

Quinoa and Crunchy Peanut Butter

Makes around 24 bites

🕐 10 minutes   📦 2 weeks   ❄ 3 months

Preparation

1. Place all the ingredients in a bowl and mix well.
2. Shape into balls, using about 1 tbsp of the mixture for each one.

Zucchini and Dark Chocolate

Makes around 24 bites

🕐 15 minutes   📦 1 week   ❄ 3 months

Preparation

1. In a food processor, process all the ingredients until combined.
2. Add the water, 1 tbsp at a time, and process until the mixture forms a ball. It should resemble the consistency of cookie dough.
3. Shape into balls, using about 1 tbsp of the mixture for each one.

Beet and White Chocolate

Makes around 20 bites

⏱ 15 minutes 📦 1 week ❄ 3 months

Preparation

① In a food processor, process all the ingredients until combined.

② Add the water, 1 tbsp at a time, and process until the mixture forms a ball. It should resemble the consistency of cookie dough.

③ Shape into balls, using about 1 tbsp of the mixture for each one.

Matcha Granola

Makes around 24 bites

🕐 10 minutes   📦 2 weeks   ❄ 3 months

Preparation

1. In a food processor, process all the ingredients until combined.
2. Shape into balls, using about 1 tbsp of the mixture for each one.

Couscous, Almond and Raisin

Makes around 24 bites

🕐 10 minutes   🗄 2 weeks   ❄ 3 months

Preparation

1. In a food processor, process all the ingredients until combined.
2. Shape into balls, using about 1 tbsp of the mixture for each one.

Fig and Five-Spice Powder

Makes around 24 bites

🕐 10 minutes   🗄 2 weeks   ❄ 3 months

Preparation

1. In a food processor, process all the ingredients until combined.
2. Shape into balls, using about 1 tbsp of the mixture for each one.

Toasted Almond, Honey and Brie

Makes around 24 bites

🕐 10 minutes   📦 1 week   ❄ 3 months

Preparation

1. In a nonstick skillet, over medium-high heat, toast the almonds, stirring constantly, for 2 minutes, until browned.
2. Place the almonds in a food processor. Add the remaining ingredients and process until combined.
3. Shape into balls, using about 1 tbsp of the mixture for each one.

Cottage Cheese and Marmalade

Makes around 24 bites

🕐 10 minutes   🗄 2 weeks   ❄ 3 months

Preparation

1. In a food processor, process all the ingredients until combined.
2. Shape into balls, using about 1 tbsp of the mixture for each one.

Rice Pudding and Raisin

Makes around 32 bites

🕐 10 minutes   📦 1 week   ❄ 3 months

Preparation

1. In a food processor, process all the ingredients until combined.
2. Shape into balls, using about 1 tbsp of the mixture for each one.

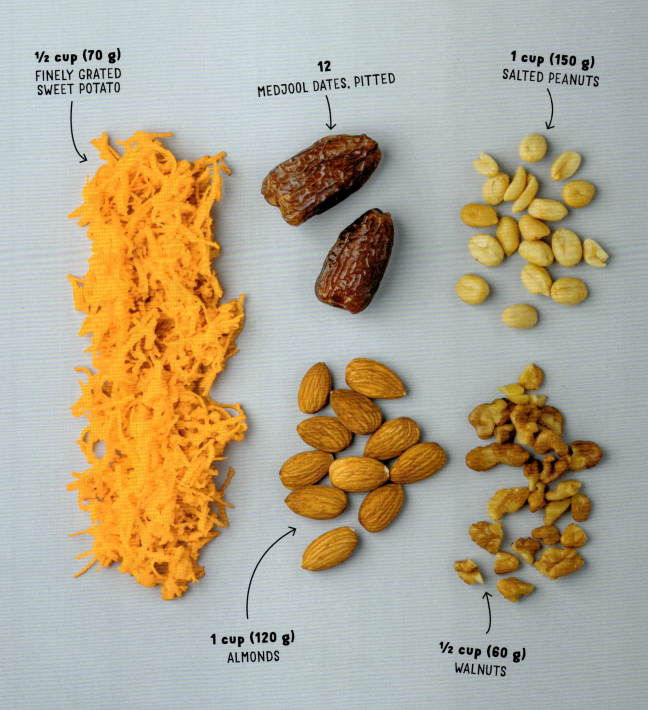

Sweet Potato and Date

Makes around 32 bites

🕐 10 minutes   🗄 1 week   ❄ 3 months

Preparation

① In a food processor, process all the ingredients until combined.

② Shape into balls, using about 1 tbsp of the mixture for each one.

Cheese and BBQ Chip

Makes around 24 bites

🕐 15 minutes   🗄 2 weeks   ❄ 3 months

Preparation

1. Place the crumbled BBQ chips in a shallow dish. Set aside.
2. Place all the remaining ingredients except the chocolate chips in a food processor.
3. Add the water, 1 tbsp at a time, and process until the mixture forms a ball. It should resemble the consistency of cookie dough.
4. Place in a large bowl, then stir in the chocolate chips.
5. Shape into balls, using about 1 tbsp of the mixture for each one. Coat evenly with the crushed BBQ chips.

Choco-Bacon

Makes around 32 bites

🕐 10 minutes 📦 1 week ❄ 3 months

Preparation

1. In a food processor, process all the ingredients until combined.
2. Shape into balls, using about 1 tbsp of the mixture for each one.

Strawberry Basil

Makes around 24 bites

🕐 15 minutes   📱 2 weeks   ❄ 3 months

Preparation

1. Place all the ingredients in a food processor.
2. Add the water, 1 tbsp at a time, and process until the mixture forms a ball. It should resemble the consistency of cookie dough.
3. Shape into balls, using about 1 tbsp of the mixture for each one.

Spicy Chocolate

Makes around 24 bites

🕐 15 minutes   📦 2 weeks   ❄ 3 months

Preparation

1. In a bowl, combine all the ingredients.
2. Shape into balls, using about 1 tbsp of the mixture for each one.

Index

Almond Flour

Baileys Coffee 111
Black Forest. 99
Blueberry Flaxseed. 39
Caramel and Fleur de Sel. 139
Carrot Cake. 107
Cashew and Pretzel 121
Cheese and BBQ Chip 177
Cherry Yogurt. 91
Choco-Sour Cream. .117
Chocolate Brownie 105
Cinnamon Bun 81
Double Chocolate. 125
Fig and Five-Spice Powder 167
Fluffy Blueberry 89
Graham Cracker 75
Multigrain 21
Piña Colada 119
Red Velvet. 127
Rum Baba 115
Strawberry Basil. 181
Toasted Coconut 77
Tofu and Toasted Sesame Seed 143
Trail Mix. 47
Vanilla Berry 67
White Bean and Cocoa. 151
Zucchini and Dark Chocolate. 159

Almonds

Almond and Coconut. 15
Almost-a-Bear-Claw .65
Baileys Coffee 111
Blueberry Flaxseed. 39
Caramel and Fleur de Sel. 139
Chocolate Brownie 105
Cinnamon Bun 81

Couscous, Almond and Raisin. 165
Dark Chocolate Almond. 49
Dried Apple and Cinnamon. 27
Graham Cracker 75
Hot Chocolate 93
Lentil and Butterscotch Chip. 153
Matcha Granola. 163
Old-Fashioned Donut 85
Pecan and Coffee 33
Puffed Rice and Marshmallow. 95
Spicy Chocolate 183
Sweet Potato and Date. 175
Tahini, Date and Honey 19
Three Nut and Creamed Honey. 53
Toasted Almond, Honey and Brie. 169
Trail Mix. 47
Zucchini and Dark Chocolate. 159

Apples

Dried Apple and Cinnamon. 27

Apricots

Oat and Apricot 31

Bacon

Choco-Bacon 179

Bananas

Banana and Yogurt. 23
Banana Bread. 61

Basil

Strawberry Basil. 181

Beans

White Bean and Cocoa. 151

Beets
Beet and White Chocolate........................161

Blueberries
Blueberry Flaxseed.............................39
Fluffy Blueberry 89
Vanilla Berry 67

Brown Sugar
Key Lime Pie 113
Piña Colada 119

Caramel
Banana Bread.................................61
Caramel and Fleur de Sel..................... 139
Lentil and Butterscotch Chip..................153
Pecan Pie 109

Carrots
Carrot Cake..................................107

Cashews
Banana Bread.................................61
Berry Center 83
Cashew and Pretzel..........................121
Crunchy Fudge...............................79
Dulce de Leche 101
Fig and Five-Spice Powder 167
Granola and Cranberry 29
Lemon Pie...................................135
Lemon Poppy Seed...........................71
Oat and Apricot 31
Pecan Pie 109
Puffed Rice and Marshmallow..................95
Three Nut and Creamed Honey.................53
Tofu Maple Walnut 145
Trail Mix 47

Cayenne Pepper
Spicy Chocolate 183

Cheese
Carrot Cake..................................107
Cheese and BBQ Chip 177
Cheesecake 103
Cinnamon Bun 81
Cottage Cheese and Marmalade...............171
Marble 59
Red Velvet...................................127
Strawberry Basil.............................181
Toasted Almond, Honey and Brie............. 169

Cherries
Black Forest..................................99
Cherry Yogurt................................91

Chia Seeds
Baileys Coffee 111
Beet and White Chocolate.....................161
Choco-Bacon 179
Choco-Sour Cream...........................117
Crunchy Fudge...............................79
Crunchy Peanut..............................73
Fresh Date and Chia Seed..................... 43
Hot Chocolate 93
Lemon Pie...................................135
Oreo Swirl...................................123
Pecan Pie 109
Puffed Rice and Marshmallow..................95
Raspberry Coconut...........................51
Strawberry Jam..............................87
Strawberry Shortcake.........................129
Toasted Sesame Seed and Dark Chocolate 35
Tofu Maple Walnut 145
Vanilla Berry 67

Chocolate

Banana and Yogurt.................................23
Beet and White Chocolate.........................161
Black Forest.......................................99
Caramel Center...................................131
Cashew and Pretzel...............................121
Cereal and Dried Fruit............................17
Cheese and BBQ Chip.............................177
Choco-Peanut Butter.............................. 63
Choco-Bacon 179
Choco-Sour Cream...............................117
Chocolate Brownie 105
Chocolate Chip 57
Crunchy Fudge....................................79
Crunchy Peanut...................................73
Dark Chocolate Almond.......................... 49
Double chocolate 125
Fig and Five-Spice Powder.......................167
Date and Chia Seed.............................. 43
Granola and Cranberry 29
Honey Nut.......................................155
Hot Chocolate....................................93
Ice Cream 133
Marble 59
Oreo Swirl.......................................123
Pumpkin seed and Dried Kiwi 45
Spicy Chocolate 183
Strawberry Basil.................................181
Strawberry Shortcake............................129
Toasted Sesame Seed and Dark Chocolate 35
Trail Mix 47
White Bean and Cocoa...........................151
Zucchini and Dark Chocolate....................159

Cinnamon

Almost-a-Bear-Claw...............................65
Cinnamon Bun....................................81
Dried Apple and Cinnamon........................27

Cocoa

Choco-Peanut Butter 63
Chocolate Brownie 105
Chocolate Cake....................................11
Chocolate Chip....................................57
Crunchy Fudge....................................79
Crunchy Peanut...................................73
Marble 59
White Bean and Cocoa...........................151

Coconut

Almond and Coconut..............................15
Piña Colada......................................119
Raspberry Coconut................................51
Toasted Coconut..................................77

Coffee

Baileys coffee....................................111
Pecan and Coffee 33

Cotton Candy

Cotton Candy....................................137

Couscous

Couscous, Almond and Raisin................... 165

Cranberries

Granola and Cranberry 29
Matcha Granola................................. 163
Multigrain 21
Toasted Almond, Honey and Brie.............. 169
Trail Mix 47

Dates

Choco-Bacon 179
Couscous, Almond and Raisin. 165
Date and Chia Seed. 43
Pistachio and Pumpkin Seed. 37
Sweet Potato and Date. 175
Tahini, Date and Honey 19
Three Nut and Creamed Honey. 53

Dried Fruit

Cereal and Dried Fruit 17
Couscous, Almond and Raisin. 165
Dried Apple and Cinnamon. 27
Granola and Cranberry 29
Matcha Granola. 163
Multigrain 21
Oat and Apricot 31
Pumpkin Seed and Dried Kiwi. 45
Quinoa and Crunchy Peanut Butter 157
Rice Pudding and Raisin. 173
Sunflower Seed and Raisin .25
Tempeh and Maple Butter. 149
Tempeh and Molasses 147
Toasted Almond, Honey and Brie. 169
Toasted Sesame Seed and Dark Chocolate 35
Tofu and Toasted Sesame Seed 143
Trail Mix. 47
Whole Grain and Dried Pineapple. 41

Dulce de Leche

Dulce de Leche 101

Figs

Fig and Five-Spice Powder. 167

Five-Spice Powder

Fig and Five-Spice Powder. 167

Flaxseed

Banana Bread. 61
Blueberry Flaxseed. 39
Caramel and Fleur de Sel. 139
Caramel Center. 131
Carrot Cake. 107
Cherry Yogurt. 91
Choco-Peanut Butter 63
Chocolate Brownie 105
Cotton Candy. 137
Granola and Cranberry. 29
Lentil and Butterscotch Chip. 153
Oat and Apricot 31
Old-Fashioned Donut 85
Rice Pudding and Raisin. 173
Sunflower Seed and Raisin .25
Tempeh and Molasses 147
Three Nut and Creamed Honey. 53
Tofu and Toasted Sesame Seed 143
White Bean and Cocoa. 151
Whole Grain and Dried Pineapple. 41

Fleur de Sel

Caramel and Fleur de Sel. 139

Ginger

Almost-a-Bear-Claw. 65
Whole Grain and Dried Pineapple. 41

Graham Cracker Crumbs

Cheesecake 103
Fluffy Blueberry 89
Graham Cracker 75
Lemon Pie. 135

Grains

Almost-a-Bear-Claw 65
Caramel Center 131
Cereal and Dried Fruit 17
Cottage Cheese and Marmalade 171
Cotton Candy 137
Dark Chocolate Almond 49
Double Chocolate 125
Granola and Cranberry 29
Honey Nut 155
Hot Chocolate 93
Ice Cream 133
Key Lime Pie 113
Matcha Granola 163
Old-Fashioned Donut 85
Oreo Swirl 123
Pecan Pie 109
Puffed Rice and Marshmallow 95
Rice Pudding and Raisin 173
Spicy Chocolate 183
Strawberry Basil 181
Strawberry Shortcake 129
Toasted Almond, Honey and Brie 169
Tofu Maple Walnut 145
Whole Grain and Dried Pineapple 41
(see also *Oats*)

Hemp Hearts

Almost-a-Bear-Claw 65
Berry Center 83
Cereal and Dried Fruit 17
Cheesecake 103
Choco-Peanut Butter 63
Chocolate Chip 57
Cottage Cheese and Marmalade 171
Cotton Candy 137
Double Chocolate 125

Fluffy Blueberry 89
Hot Chocolate 93
Ice Cream 133
Key Lime Pie 113
Lemon Poppy Seed 71
Matcha Granola 163
Multigrain 21
Old-Fashioned Donut 85
Pecan and Coffee 33
Piña Colada 119
Pistachio and Pumpkin Seed 37
Pistachio Mint 69
Raspberry Coconut 51
Red Velvet 127
Strawberry Basil 181
Toasted Almond, Honey and Brie 169
Toasted Coconut 77
Zucchini and Dark Chocolate 159

Honey

Almond and Coconut 15
Blueberry Flaxseed 39
Carrot Cake 107
Cashew and Pretzel 121
Cereal and Dried Fruit 17
Cheese and BBQ Chip 177
Cheesecake 103
Cherry Yogurt 91
Dark Chocolate Almond 49
Dried Apple and Cinnamon 27
Fig and Five-Spice Powder 167
Fluffy Blueberry 89
Graham Cracker 75
Honey Nut 155
Lemon Poppy Seed 71
Lentil and Butterscotch Chip 153
Marble 59

Matcha Granola.....................................163
Multigrain 21
Pecan and Coffee 33
Pumpkin Seed and Dried Kiwi....................45
Quinoa and Crunchy Peanut Butter 157
Raspberry Coconut................................51
Red Velvet...127
Rum Baba 115
Spicy Chocolate 183
Sunflower Seed and Raisin 25
Tahini, Date and Honey 19
Three Nut and Creamed Honey.................53
Toasted Almond, Honey and Brie............. 169
Toasted Coconut 77
Toasted Sesame Seed and Dark Chocolate 35
Tofu and Toasted Sesame Seed 143
Vanilla Berry 67
Whole Grain and Dried Pineapple..............41

Kiwi
Pumpkin Seed and Dried Kiwi....................45

Lemon
Lemon Pie..135
Lemon Poppy Seed................................71

Lentils
Lentil and Butterscotch Chip....................153

Lime
Key Lime Pie 113

Mango
Toasted Sesame Seed and Dark Chocolate 35

Maple Syrup or Butter
Berry Center....................................... 83
Chocolate Brownie 105
Chocolate Chip....................................57
Cinnamon Bun 81
Crunchy Peanut....................................73
Granola and Cranberry...........................29
Old-Fashioned Donut 85
Pistachio Mint..................................... 69
Tempeh and Maple Butter...................... 149
Tofu Maple Walnut 145

Marmalade
Cottage Cheese and Marmalade................171

Marshmallow Cream
Puffed Rice and Marshmallow....................95

Matcha
Matcha Granola.................................. 163

Mint
Pistachio Mint..................................... 69

Molasses
Almost-a-Bear-Claw...............................65
Tempeh and Molasses 147

Nutmeg
Carrot Cake.......................................107
Multigrain 21

Oats
Almond and Coconut..............................15
Banana and Yogurt................................23
Banana Bread......................................61
Berry Center....................................... 83

Blueberry Flaxseed.............................39
Cereal and Dried Fruit 17
Cherry Yogurt................................91
Choco-Peanut Butter 63
Chocolate Chip 57
Cinnamon Bun 81
Crunchy Fudge...............................79
Crunchy Peanut...............................73
Dark Chocolate Almond........................49
Date and Chia Seed...........................43
Dried Apple and Cinnamon....................27
Dulce de Leche 101
Lemon Poppy Seed............................71
Lentil and Butterscotch Chip...................153
Marble....................................59
Oat and Apricot 31
Pecan and Coffee 33
Pistachio Mint...............................69
Pumpkin Seed and Dried Kiwi..................45
Quinoa and Crunchy Peanut Butter 157
Raspberry Coconut...........................51
Rice Pudding and Raisin......................173
Spicy Chocolate 183
Strawberry Jam 87
Sunflower Seed and Raisin 25
Tahini, Date and Honey.......................19
Tempeh and Maple Butter.....................149
Tempeh and Molasses 147
Toasted Sesame Seed and Dark Chocolate 35
Tofu and Toasted Sesame Seed...............143
Vanilla Berry 67
Whole Grain and Dried Pineapple...............41

Oreo Cookies
Oreo Swirl..................................123

Peanuts
Beet and White Chocolate.....................161
Caramilk Center 131
Cereal and Dried Fruit 17
Choco-Peanut Butter 63
Choco-Sour Cream...........................117
Chocolate Chip 57
Crunchy Peanut...............................73
Date and Chia Seed...........................43
Honey Nut.................................155
Oat and Apricot 31
Oreo Swirl.................................123
Quinoa and Crunchy Peanut Butter 157
Sunflower Seed and Raisin 25
Sweet Potato and Date.......................175
Tempeh and Molasses 147
Toasted Sesame Seed and Dark Chocolate 35
White Bean and Cocoa........................151

Pecans
Beet and White Chocolate.....................161
Choco-Bacon 179
Cottage Cheese and Marmalade................171
Fig and Five-Spice Powder....................167
Pecan and Coffee 33
Pecan Pie 109
Rice Pudding and Raisin......................173
Spicy Chocolate 183
Three Nut and Creamed Honey.................53

Pineapple
Piña Colada 119
Whole Grain and Dried Pineapple...............41

Pistachios
Choco-Bacon 179
Lemon Pie.................................135

Matcha Granola.................................163
Pistachio and Pumpkin Seed....................37
Pistachio Mint.................................69
Tempeh and Maple Butter.....................149

Poppy Seeds
Banana and Yogurt.............................23
Berry Center...................................83
Cereal and Dried Fruit........................17
Granola and Cranberry.........................29
Lemon Poppy Seed.............................71

Potato Chips
Cheese and BBQ Chip..........................177

Pretzels
Cashew and Pretzel............................121

Pumpkin Seeds
Multigrain....................................21
Pistachio and Pumpkin Seed....................37
Pumpkin Seed and Dried Kiwi...................45
Tahini, Date and Honey........................19

Quinoa
Quinoa and Crunchy Peanut Butter............157

Raisins
Couscous, Almond and Raisin..................165
Quinoa and Crunchy Peanut Butter............157
Rice Pudding and Raisin.......................173
Sunflower Seed and Raisin.....................25
Tempeh and Molasses.........................147
Tofu and Toasted Sesame Seed...............143

Raspberries
Berry Center...................................83
Raspberry Coconut.............................51
Vanilla Berry..................................67

Rum
Rum Baba....................................115

Sesame Seeds
Multigrain....................................21
Toasted Sesame Seed and Dark Chocolate....35
Tofu and Toasted Sesame Seed...............143
(see also *Tahini*)

Sour Cream
Choco-Sour Cream............................117
Key Lime Pie.................................113

Strawberries
Strawberry Basil...............................181
Strawberry Jam................................87
Strawberry Shortcake.........................129

Sunflower Seeds
Fig and Five-Spice Powder....................167
Multigrain....................................21
Sunflower Seed and Raisin.....................25
Trail Mix......................................47

Sweet Potato
Sweet Potato and Date........................175

Tahini
Double Chocolate.............................125
Fluffy Blueberry..............................89
Pumpkin Seed and Dried Kiwi...................45
Strawberry Jam................................87

Tahini, Date and Honey 19
Tofu and Toasted Sesame Seed 143

Tea
Matcha Granola 163

Tempeh
Tempeh and Maple Butter 149
Tempeh and Molasses 147

Tofu
Tofu and Toasted Sesame Seed 143
Tofu Maple Walnut 145

Vanilla
Baileys Coffee 111
Beet and White Chocolate 161
Caramel and Fleur de Sel 139
Carrot Cake 107
Cheese and BBQ Chip 177
Cheesecake 103
Cinnamon Bun 81
Cotton Candy 137
Dulce de Leche 101
Ice Cream 133
Key Lime Pie 113
Lemon Pie 135
Marble 59
Pecan Pie 109
Piña Colada 119
Pistachio and Pumpkin Seed .37
Raspberry Center 83

Red Velvet 127
Rum Baba 115
Strawberry Basil 181
Strawberry Shortcake 129
Vanilla Berry 67
Vanilla Cake 9

Walnuts
Banana and Yogurt 23
Banana Bread 61
Carrot Cake 107
Chocolate Brownie 105
Crunchy Fudge 79
Honey Nut 155
Sweet Potato and Date 175
Tofu Maple Walnut 145
Trail Mix 47

Wheat Germ
Marble 59
Whole Grain and Dried Pineapple 41

Yogurt
Banana and Yogurt 23
Cherry Yogurt 91
Graham Cracker 75

Zucchini
Zucchini and Dark Chocolate 159